The Secret Life of Puppies

PAVILION

The Secret Life of Puppies

A dog's-eye view of its first year of life

CONTENTS

INTRODUCTION

A puppy is born every minute in the UK, and we are a nation of self-confessed puppy lovers. Buying a puppy is one of the most exciting and rewarding experiences you can have. Puppies are cute, fun, loving and intelligent – but they can also be frustrating, mischievous and the greatest time-wasters on earth! Dogs pee, poo, bark, chew, dig, run, jump, chase and bite. They can behave in ways that most humans find hard to understand – or even totally baffling!

The Secret Life of Puppies offers an intriguing insight into those first few weeks and months of life, as puppies change from blind, deaf and toothless youngsters, totally dependent on their mother and litter mates for warmth, into confident canines full of their own very special charisma. By understanding why they behave in the way that they do and how they try to communicate with us, you'll be well on the way to building a special relationship with your very best friend.

Throughout the book you will also find special features such as training exercises, healthcare checks and troubleshooting tips for those times when things aren't quite going according to plan. You'll also meet some of the adorable puppies featured in the series and find out more about those particular breeds.

The first weeks and months of owning a puppy offer a chance for you to shape your pet's behaviour and character for the rest of his or her life. This period is fun and exciting – but it goes so fast! Whatever the breed or type of your puppy, enjoy these early days and make the most of them. Welcome to the world of dogs!

CHOOSING THE RIGHT DOG FOR YOU

Many people choose their dog for its looks, and there's nothing wrong with using that as a starting point. But you also need to be sure that your dog will suit your home and lifestyle. Here's a checklist of questions to ask yourself:

- ❧ What size of dog do you want — a small dog that will happily sit on your lap, such as a Bichon Frise, or a large one like a St Bernard?
- ❧ How much space do you have, both indoors and outdoors? If you live in a small flat, then a Newfoundland isn't going to be your best choice!
- ❧ Who lives in your home? Some dogs are very big and could more easily knock down a child or someone who is elderly or infirm.
- ❧ How much time can you spend exercising your dog? A Border Collie, for example, will need to be taken for a walk two or three times a day. Will your job and lifestyle allow you to do that?

- ❀ How much time can you spend on grooming? A short-haired Greyhound won't need much attention, but an Afghan Hound is seriously high maintenance.
- ❀ How strong is the dog you're thinking of buying? Can you physically handle it?
- ❀ How much food does it need? Feeding a large dog can send your shopping bills sky high.
- ❀ Have you factored in the cost of vaccinations, pet insurance and vets' bills?
- ❀ Is the breed you're interested in prone to any particular health problems? Some breeds suffer from serious health and welfare problems that can impact their quality of life.

By now you should have whittled your selection down to a small number of breeds. Before you go any further, speak to people who already own an adult of the breed you're thinking of buying. If possible, get some hands-on experience such as taking their dog for a walk (remember to take a poop scoop! It's not pleasant, but it's an essential part of being a responsible dog owner), being present at feeding time or watching them in a training session.

PEDIGREE OR CROSSBREED?

In recent years there has been an explosion in the number of deliberate first-crosses between recognised breeds. Mixes such as Cockerpoos (Cocker Spaniel and Miniature Poodle) and Puggles (Pug/Beagle crosses) now outrank pedigree breeds in many areas. They can make wonderful pets: often the best of the two breeds' characteristics come to the fore, but this is not guaranteed, even in the same litter! For example, although Poodle crosses can create dogs with coats that do not shed, this is not always the case. So if you opt for a first-cross puppy, do be prepared for it to look and behave both the same and differently from its parents!

Pedigree dogs are bred to a breed standard. This means that you will be able to accurately predict how large your dog will be as an adult.

Viewing a litter

Having decided on the breed of dog that you want, your next task is to find a litter of puppies to choose from. Now you're getting to the exciting bit — meeting a bunch of cute, energetic puppies face to face! This is the point where you need to make sure you don't let your heart rule your head. When you go to view them, these are the things to look out for:

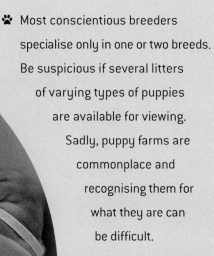

❧ Most conscientious breeders specialise only in one or two breeds. Be suspicious if several litters of varying types of puppies are available for viewing. Sadly, puppy farms are commonplace and recognising them for what they are can be difficult.

❧ Ask the breeder if he or she uses The Puppy Contract, which is endorsed by major animal welfare and veterinary organisations. Go to puppycontract.rspca.org.uk/home for more information.

❧ The breeder should ask you many questions about your home and family life. Good breeders care about where their puppies live and want them to have a happy life with the same household forever. Unscrupulous breeders are often more interested in how you are going to pay than in how you are going to look after their pup.

* Walk away if the conditions are dirty or the breeder tries to persuade you to pay for and take a puppy (or two) there and then.

* Never buy a puppy from a pet shop or a dealer. Sadly, such puppies may have been separated from their mother far too early, and may have had seriously deprived rearing, both physically and mentally.

* Nearly all pedigree dogs require physical checks before they are mated, to ensure that they do not pass on unwanted hereditary defects. Find out what defects exist in the breed you like and ask the Kennel Club to tell you which checks the stud dog and bitch should have had before breeding.

* Look at the litter as a whole. They should be bright-eyed and active and free of any obvious health problems.

* Of course, all puppies need to sleep a great deal. If you arrive during a siesta, you may need to return an hour or so later to be able to view them when they are awake.

* The puppies should be with their mother. This is because the mother's state of health and behaviour will be a very good indicator as to how the puppies will behave later in life. If the mother is aggressive, walk away.

- The puppies should all be active and energetic. Eight-week-old puppies do need a lot of rest, but on waking they need to relieve themselves and then get on with the serious business of playing and exploring.

- On the whole, the best choice for most families is the average puppy – one that is not shy, but is likely to be confident enough to be able to cope with the busy routine of everyday life. This pup may not be the first to climb on to your lap, but he will be keen to explore and to meet you. If you clap your hands, he may move away if startled, but will quickly return to see what the noise was. If held carefully, he should not struggle too much, but will be happy to be petted and touched before being returned to play with his litter mates.

- Discount any puppy that sits despondently at the back, refusing to come forward, is fearful of being held or handled, shies away from noises or is defensive towards other puppies.

- Don't be downhearted if you are not given a free choice from all the pups in the litter. Breeders often keep a puppy for themselves, or they may have already allocated particular puppies to their new owners.

NEWBORNS

From birth to 4 weeks

0–13 DAYS

the neonatal period

What could be more adorable —or more vulnerable — than a newborn puppy? Blind and deaf (their ears and eyes won't open until they are two to three weeks old), these soft-haired, squirming little bundles cannot even breathe freely until their mother has licked them clean of their birth membrane. They cannot even pee or poo by themselves; their mother licks them to stimulate them to do so, and she will usually eat the waste to keep the nest site clean.

Although it won't be long before they're tottering and tumbling all over the place, newborn puppies are unable to support their own weight and so they crawl over each other with paddling motions on their front legs. This helps to develop both their muscles and their co-ordination. They won't be able to regulate their own body temperature until they are between seven and ten days old, so newborn pups huddle together and lie close to their mother to share body heat.

Unable to see or hear, newborn pups detect their mother's body heat and locate her teats through a combination of heat receptors and smell receptors, all of which are located in the puppy's nose. Indeed, a puppy's nose seems to take up a disproportionate amount of its face!

DID YOU KNOW...?

During the neonatal period, an average litter will eat for approximately 30 per cent of the time and sleep for the rest!

MUM'S MILK

The milk that the mother produces in the first 24 hours after giving birth is known as colostrum; it contains a highly concentrated mix of antibodies, as well as water, vitamins, electrolytes and nutrients, which gives puppies protection from infection and disease. Towards the end of the puppies' first 18 hours of life they lose the ability to absorb the antibodies, so it's essential that puppies nurse successfully from their mother in those first few hours.

Puppy talk

At just one day old, many puppies can already make several different noises such as whining, mewing, grunting and even screaming. These noises alert the mother if a puppy strays too far from the nest, is in pain or distress or is being squashed. At one week old, puppies are likely to be able to add yelps to this list. It is almost impossible for the pups' mother to ignore these cries. Most mothers will even leave the nest to follow a tape recording of her puppies if it is played back, even at some distance from her.

Getting used to people

Although puppies are blind and deaf at this stage, their sense of smell is already active and they can feel a certain amount, too — so they can start becoming familiar with all things human straight away. Puppies can be held very gently for short periods of time, which allows physical checks to be made and the puppy's weight monitored, while at the same time giving the puppy a chance to get used to being handled and touched.

WEEKS 2–4

the transitional phase

The next stage of the puppy's life is known as the transitional phase, because so many changes are taking place in both physical development and behaviour. In the third week of life, puppies' ears open and their eyes can focus on light and moving objects, although neither of these two senses will be fully functioning until around five weeks of age.

Puppies of three weeks can crawl backwards as well as forwards, but will try to walk now, rather than crawl. This means they are now able to move away from the nest to urinate and defecate, and are no longer reliant on their mother to help them eliminate waste matter from their bodies.

At four weeks of age, the puppies start teething. Just like human children, puppies have two sets of teeth – one deciduous set and a permanent set that replace these at around 18–22 weeks of age. As soon as the first set of teeth arrives, puppies start to put things in their mouths to experiment with them; food, objects, each other and even mum's tail may find their way into their mouths and play becomes a much more important part of their day.

The arrival of sharp puppy teeth starts the weaning process (see page 44), where the mother begins to restrict how often and for how long the puppies may suckle. Puppies can now learn to lap milk from a dish.

PUPPY PROGRESS

Based on a medium-sized mongrel, this is your puppy's development rate compared to that of a human child.

PUPPY	CHILD
2–4 weeks	1–2 years
4–8 weeks	3–4 years
8–12 weeks	5–7 years
12–18 weeks	8–11 years
5–9 months	11–14 years
9–12 months	15–17 years

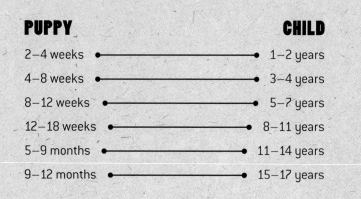

Playtime!

It's at this age that puppies start to behave like dogs! They can walk and even attempt to run and jump – usually on each other! Pups can now bark, wag their tails and will bite at each other in play. Although they still spend a great deal of time sleeping, their waking hours will now be filled with feeding from their mother when she permits, feeding from a dish as they start to be able to eat solid food, and playing and exploring.

PICKING UP A PUPPY

Puppies can be incredibly wriggly! Here's how to do it safely.

1

Place one hand underneath the pup's chest, cradling this area and putting your fingers between his front legs.

2

Scoop the puppy from underneath with your other hand and support his bottom. You can then lift the puppy onto a surface or your lap. If you are carrying him, tuck him well into your chest.

3

Take particular care when putting the puppy back down. Make sure that you keep a firm hold until you can feel that his body weight is back on the floor. Pups sometimes try to jump when they see the floor is within reach and this can cause an accident if you do not have a firm hold.

Learning all the time

One of the most important ways in which puppies learn is by watching and imitating their mother. This means that if the mother is anxious or aggressive, the pups could learn to be this way, too – whereas if she is calm, friendly and relaxed, then the pups are likely to copy her.

Puppies also learn a great deal through playing with each other and by exploring the world around them. Aspects of their environment can now be made more challenging by adding toys, objects to climb on and fall over, and even textured surfaces, so that the puppies become accustomed to walking on different kinds of flooring. Of course, puppies of this age are rather clumsy and will often slide over on slippery surfaces, fall off the lowest platform and tumble into each other in play. This all helps to give them confidence; puppies that are not allowed to romp and behave in this normal way may grow up to be inhibited or anxious as adults.

Handling is now even more important. Puppies need to be able to have contact with people – and lots of them – if they are to grow into well-adjusted and confident dogs later on. Encourage adults of all descriptions and children to see the pups and play with them at this stage and beyond. Sadly, all too many puppies lead an over-sheltered life and can show fear of unknown people as adults if they have not been given sufficient exposure to humans at this stage of their life.

Puppies also need to experience the sounds of the world around them, to that they don't grown up to be fearful of unexpected or unusual sounds. In a domestic environment, most puppies will be automatically exposed to the many different sounds of daily life. Hearing human voices, the TV and radio will familiarise them with the noises people make, while the sound of washing machines, vacuum cleaners and saucepans clattering in the kitchen will all help them adjust easily when they move to their new home.

PUPPY LOVE

(RELATIONSHIPS WITH HUMANS AND OTHER PUPPIES)

Scientists believe that domestic dogs have evolved to form strong attachments to humans as part of their social development. This need to have a bond with people is what makes our pet dogs so unique in the animal world, and means that they have a deep psychological desire to be with us, have contact, and enjoy our company. Research has shown that dogs can 'read' human faces – and most especially our emotions – in a way that no other non-human animal can, and this makes them sensitive to our moods and feelings, sometimes even when we are unaware of them ourselves.

Puppies learn about how humans behave from experience, but they also come into the world with a remarkable potential to understand and engage with us — for example, they seem to inherently understand that a human smile is a good thing — even though we show our teeth, which in the dog world might be interpreted as a threat.

MEET

Ace, the Corgi

Ace is a very confident, independent little chap and happy in his own company, although he hasn't met a single person, animal or object he hasn't instantly liked. He's very fond of his toy Cuddly Monkey and he takes it to bed every night. Ace's other favourite chew toys include a plastic funnel and a dustpan and brush (not that he helps with the tidying). He loves to chill out in the doorway of his home with his back legs out like a frog and his front legs tucked in underneath him.

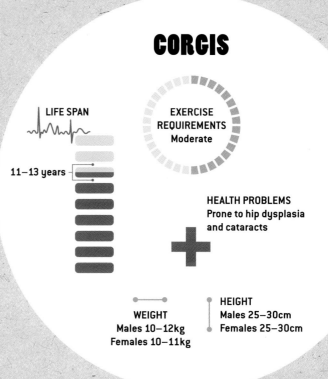

CORGIS

LIFE SPAN
11–13 years

EXERCISE REQUIREMENTS
Moderate

HEALTH PROBLEMS
Prone to hip dysplasia and cataracts

WEIGHT
Males 10–12kg
Females 10–11kg

HEIGHT
Males 25–30cm
Females 25–30cm

YOUR DOG AT HOME

4–8 weeks

PHYSICAL CHANGES

In this phase, physical growth is also highly apparent and puppies begin to look more robust and stronger. Refinements to facial features mean that their heads and muzzles look more in proportion and, as muscles develop, they are able to show more subtle facial expressions. Ear positions are more mobile and varied, and the pup will pull his lips back in a 'smile', or push them forwards to show likes and dislikes, as well as enjoyment, appeasement and possession of items. This phase is very much about social experimentation and that also means that the pup will 'practise' many physical moves and positions, including stalking, pouncing, biting and shaking items in his mouth, and even mounting.

LEARNING TO BE A DOG

Around five weeks of age, a pup's brain waves are the same as those of an adult dog – meaning that, even though their stamina and concentration span may be limited, the pups' capacity for learning is not. Coming when called for food, learning how to communicate with other puppies in the litter and learning from mum are all possible. At this stage, the puppy is like a little sponge, absorbing all the information that it is exposed to.

By now, most puppies are beginning to practise the kinds of behaviours that they will need as adults. Puppies of four to five weeks can growl, chase moving objects, shake objects as if they were killing them and play rough games with each other, during which they start to learn how to inhibit the strength of their biting. Pups of both sexes will also engage in mounting behaviours now. This is not necessarily sexual, but is simply an opportunity to practise a social body posture in play and to experiment.

DID YOU KNOW...?

Puppies can be seen to dream from about five weeks' onwards. It's thought that this is part of their neural development – although what they dream about will always remain a mystery.

DID YOU KNOW...?

In one study, Chihuahua puppies were raised with kittens between the ages of four and eight weeks; they were then found to prefer the company of cats after this time, and didn't even seem to recognise their own species when exposed to other dogs! This is why encouraging puppies to socialise with both other dogs and humans is so important.

NEW
EXPERIENCES

Most puppies stay with their mother, in the breeder's home, until they are seven to eight weeks of age. During this time, they need to be handled by as many different people as possible, to become used to the smell and touch of humans and to form bonds with them – although this should be done in a controlled way, for short periods of time, so that the puppy does not feel overwhelmed or frightened. Pups also need to be able to play with members of their own species; singleton pups may miss out if they do not have canine companionship.

Pups also need to be able to take in as many different sights and experiences as possible at this age. Even putting the pups in the car and taking them for a short ride will help them to acclimatise to this unusual experience. Meeting other vaccinated, friendly, adult dogs – and even cats – will also be a big bonus. Most importantly, a short period of individual handling for each puppy several times a day will mean that they get used to being with people rather than depending on the company of their litter mates and mother. This will prepare them for leaving home.

WEANING

For the first month of life, puppies depend entirely on their mother's milk. She will stay with her litter for the majority of the day and night and will roll onto one side to expose her teats so that the pups can suckle at will.

At around four to five weeks of age, the weaning process starts and the puppies begin taking solid food. What triggers this to happen? The short answer is that suckling hurts! It's around this time that puppies begin to get their 'baby teeth'. Having eight or nine clamouring puppies all attempting to grab a teat with razor-sharp teeth at the same time must be distinctly uncomfortable!

Suddenly, the rules change. The mother spends longer amounts of time away from the puppies, which results in her being 'mobbed' by hungry pups on her return. After a while, most bitches tend to simply get up and walk away. The pups become frustrated and try even harder to reach their mother and latch on. As they try harder to get to her, the bitch will need to redirect their demands for food to another source – from a bowl of food in our domestic setting.

DINNER TIME

Weaning is designed
to encourage the pups to start to
find their own food, and this means learning
to eat solids. Lapping liquid foods from a dish is usually
the first part of the process. Not long after, puppies will take
solid food from a dish and will try to eat it — although some may
well be justly accused of playing with their food to begin with!

Feeding several puppies all at once can be a gloriously messy affair, but
it is very important that the breeder supervises mealtimes and makes
sure that each puppy has its share by providing individual feeding
dishes rather than one large platter. This is because sharing
food can increase competition between puppies and can
sometimes lead to food guarding later in life.

Until the pups realise this, good mothers make their displeasure at their puppies' repeated attempts to feed known in firm, but gentle ways. A hard stare is the pups' first warning. A growl may follow. Very persistent puppies may then be subjected to a nose-butt, where they are pushed firmly away, or even an inhibited snap, where the bitch snaps her jaws close to the puppy without making contact.

Puppies are not born knowing what a hard stare or even a growl means. Sensitive puppies work things out very quickly and soon give up trying to feed if their mother gives them that 'look'. More determined puppies, however, may push their mothers to the limit.

Eventually, all the puppies learn that when their mother returns to them they need to lick her around the mouth and face, rather than her underbelly, to solicit food and attention. Interestingly, nearly all dogs retain the basic greeting behaviours learned as a tiny puppy and even as adults will greet other dogs and people by sniffing and licking at their mouths and faces.

PREPARING TO BRING YOUR NEW PUPPY HOME

Most puppies join their new families at around seven to eight weeks of age. The more preparation you can do in advance, the more quickly your puppy will settle in. Here's a checklist of things to do before you bring him home.

❧ Ring your local vet and find out when your puppy should have his vaccinations (see page 60) – and book an appointment.

❧ Ring your local puppy class and ask if you can come to watch before you sign up.

❧ Make sure that your garden is secure. As soon as you get your new puppy home, you will probably want to take him straight into the garden to relieve himself – and this is not the time to discover that there are holes in your fencing!

❧ Puppies will sniff, chew and lick almost anything. Make sure that any potential hazards (such as electric cables or fragile ornaments) and toxic substances (such as cleaning solutions or medicines) are well out of reach and slug pellets and flower bulbs, that are poisonous to dogs, are removed from the garden.

- Buy a supply of the same food that has been given by the breeder. Puppies are easily prone to stomach upsets and a change of food can create havoc with their digestive system and, subsequently, with their house training.

- Ensure you have separate water and feeding dishes for your puppy.

- Decide where your puppy is going to sleep. There are many beds available, but a cardboard box with a warm blanket in a quiet area will do just as well to start with. Ideally, bring a towel or piece of blanket home with you from the breeder. This cloth will carry the comforting scent of the puppy's mother and brothers and sisters.

- Do you have other animals to consider? Cats need a high place to escape to, while pet rabbits and guinea pigs will need secure penning.

- Buy a lightweight, comfortable puppy collar and lead. Choke chains or other 'correctional' collars should never be used.

TRAINING EXERCISE 1

House training

The breeder may already have started house training your pup by the time you bring him home – but if not, this is the definitely the first bit of training you'll want to do! Learn to predict when your puppy will need to go to the toilet – after playing, after waking up, after any kind of excitement, such as the children coming home from school, and straight after meals. At these times, take your puppy to the same place outside and wait with him – even in the rain. As soon as your puppy starts to sniff around, or circle, praise him very gently. Once he has relieved himself, lavish him with praise and give him a really special tit-bit as a reward.

In between times, take your puppy outside about once an hour, just in case he should need to go, and also to watch him closely for signs that he might need to go, such as sniffing or circling.

If your puppy does not go to the toilet, bring him back inside. At this point you know that he is likely to need to go in the next hour. If you cannot supervise him during that time, put him in a crate or play pen, or in an enclosed area where you do not mind if he has an accident. Most dogs do not want to soil their sleeping area, and will therefore try to wait until you take them out again.

If you catch your puppy in the act of going, or about to go, at any another time, say 'Outside' in an urgent tone of voice, then take him quickly outside to show him where you do want him to go – even if it's too late to save your carpet! If you get even one drop in the right place, you can then praise your puppy.

Being cross with your puppy for making a mistake in the house is pointless. Dogs soon learn to associate any mess with your anger – not with the act of going – and simply show fear when you find it – or worse, learn to eat their own excrement. Never, ever use an old-fashioned punishment such as rubbing the dog's nose in its own mess.

PUPPY TALK

Weaning (and understanding the warning signals that the mother gives to discourage her pups from feeding at will) is the first stage in puppies learning the meaning of other dogs' body language – in effect, how to 'speak dog'.

You too can learn to understand some of the expressions that make up canine language.

EARS

Dogs put their ears back when they are feeling anxious – in this instance, they are usually flat to the head. However, they may also put their ears back to show friendliness, in which case, you will often see the inside of each ear.

EYES

Dogs squint and blink when they are trying to be non-threatening – either because they are being friendly or because they are anxious.

FOREHEAD

Just like humans, dogs furrow their brows when they are worried or when they are focusing intently on something with great concentration. (Of course, some breeds, such as Boxers and Shar-Peis, have an almost permanently furrowed brow, so this needs to be taken into account.)

TAIL

Tail wagging means that a dog is happy, doesn't it? Well, not always. For dogs, tail wagging is as much about disseminating scent information as it is about visual signals, so the speed and position of the tail itself matter, too. Low, fast tail wags nearly always indicate uncertainty, whereas horizontal, open wags generally demonstrate friendliness. Indeed, some dogs wag so enthusiastically that their tails go round in a 'windmill' style.

MOUTH

Most dogs keep their teeth deliberately concealed when they are being friendly, as this is polite in canine communication. Lip licking and yawning can both be signs of stress, which are worth watching out for in your dog.

BODY

Confident dogs carry their weight four square, while anxious or fearful ones will lower their bodies towards the ground and shift their body weight well away from whatever is worrying them.

MEET

Molly, the English Pointer

Molly is incredibly intelligent. When she first moved to her new home she learned how to open her family's sensor bin in the kitchen. She would activate the lid to open, allowing her to ransack the wastage and leftover food. Her family decided to turn the bin the other way round and to Molly's dismay she could no longer eat last night's dinner. When Molly's not poking her head into the bin, she's chewing her favourite toy Fox and eating like a queen with homemade liver cake. She has a very affectionate side and loves cuddling up to her family on the sofa.

ENGLISH POINTERS

LIFE SPAN

13–14 years

EXERCISE REQUIREMENTS
High

HEALTH PROBLEMS
Prone to hip dysplasia and thyroid problems

WEIGHT
Males 24–34kg
Females 20–28kg

HEIGHT
Males 55–62cm
Females 54–60cm

PHYSICAL DEVELOPMENT

8–12 weeks

INTO
EVERYTHING!

By eight weeks, the pups' limbs should be sturdy and beginning to develop muscle, their appetites healthy and their eyes full of inquisitive mischief. Puppies can run, jump, pounce and trot, just like adult dogs, although obviously their stamina and strength is still being developed. Young joints can be accidentally put under stress at this stage and you must take care not to over-exercise puppies under the age of nine months to a year, to avoid joint problems later on. It's also best not to let them do excessive stair climbing or repeated standing on their hind legs.

At this stage, puppies are into everything! Their desire to explore can get them into trouble if they are not supervised and their need to chew can also be hazardous if they are not carefully directed onto appropriate chew toys. Their needle-sharp teeth are used to explore objects and other animals – including us! This is completely normal and is a valuable part of the pup's education, as he will be learning how hard he can bite living creatures. Puppies start this learning process in the litter through play biting other puppies, but many then miss out on further education with other puppies until they have finished their vaccination programmes at the age of 12–14 weeks. If this is the case with your puppy, then try to compensate for it as far as possible; early vaccination (see page 60) and a good puppy class can both help.

Puppies of this age should be going out into the world to meet as many different people, other dogs, animals and experiences as possible. Waiting for the pup's vaccinations to be complete will be too late. Do make sure that these are positive experiences, however, don't take him into a potentially frightening environment, such as a fireworks display or a crowded shopping centre, in the hope that he'll get used to it.

YOUR PUPPY'S FIRST VACCINATIONS

Your vet will start your puppy on a course of vaccinations against the four main infectious diseases – canine distemper, hepatitis, leptospirosis and parvovirus. You may also want to have your dog vaccinated against kennel cough; your vet can advise you on this. All of these diseases can be fatal, so after its first course of vaccinations, your puppy will need to be re-vaccinated every year.

Puppies generally receive their first vaccinations from approximately eight weeks of age, although (depending on your vet), they can receive them earlier, with the first injection being given at six weeks and the second at ten weeks.

Until your puppy is fully vaccinated, do not take him anywhere where he might come into contact with dogs or ground that may be infected. However, you can allow him to mix with other adult dogs as long as you know that these dogs are up to date with their own vaccinations.

TOP TIP

KEEP YOUR DOG'S VACCINATION CERTIFICATES SAFE, AS YOU MAY NEED TO SHOW THEM IF YOU TAKE YOUR DOG TO BOARDING KENNELS OR OVERSEAS.

OUT IN THE BIG, WIDE WORLD

Puppies usually move to their new home between seven and eight weeks of age, so this is a momentous time for them – so many strange new places to explore and people to meet! And if moving house is stressful for humans, imagine what it must be like for a puppy! Away from its mother and litter mates for the first time, faced with strange sights, sounds and smells, it's not surprising that most puppies feel a little daunted to begin with. The more preparation you can do in advance, the more quickly your puppy will settle in his new home.

DO

🐾 Make sure your puppy has a comfy, cosy bed of his own. A crate or indoor kennel is ideal.

🐾 Practice 'sleeping arrangements' during the day. Puppies often sleep badly on their first few nights in a new home simply because their sleeping area is unfamiliar. Every time your puppy looks sleepy during the day, pick him up and place him where you want him to sleep at night. Then leave him there. If he whines or cries, wait a few minutes to see if he settles down of his own accord; if he doesn't, you may need to gradually wean him off human company.

🐾 Make sure your puppy has been out to the toilet before bedtime. Be prepared to get up in the night to take your puppy out to relieve himself in the first few nights – or at the very least to get up early and make this a priority.

DON'T

🐾 Don't be tempted to take your new puppy into the bed with you, or allow your children to do so. Your puppy will come to depend on the close contact and will expect this to happen for ever.

🐾 Don't shout at or be cross with your puppy if he is keeping you awake by barking, howling or whining. He's only doing it because he feels insecure and any apparent aggression from you will only make it worse.

PUPPIES AND YOUNG CHILDREN

It's sometimes been said that the only difference between puppies and young children is the number of legs! If you're bringing a young pup into a household where there are children, you need to establish some basic ground rules from the outset to ensure that they all get along.

Puppies tire easily, and once fatigue sets in they can behave like petulant toddlers themselves, becoming irritable and even snappy. Interaction needs to be short and sweet, and the puppy must have a quiet place to sleep undisturbed. Crates or indoor kennels are ideal, as the puppy can be safely inside, with a lock on the door to keep prying little fingers away.

Children of all ages need to learn how to stroke and handle a puppy correctly, by tickling them on the chest and tummy, rather than bending over the top of the head, which may be perceived as a threat.

Children also need to learn that putting their faces or hair up close to a puppy's face is an invitation for the puppy to play bite them. While the puppy may not mean to cause harm, their sharp teeth can do considerable damage. Rough-and-tumble games can also lead to over-excitement and the risk of tears before bedtime. Hide-and-seek games with a toy, training games and retrieving games are far safer and more appropriate.

PUPPIES AND OLDER DOGS

Perhaps you already have an older dog? Ideally, introduce the two to each other on neutral territory — in the garden, or even at the breeder's home. Keep your older dog on a lead, but allow him to sniff the puppy. Most adult dogs are excellent with pups, but if you are unsure how yours will react be cautious to start with.

Once the initial greetings are over, lead your adult dog into the house first, allowing the pup to follow. Give your older dog lots of praise and attention, even if this means ignoring the pup for a while. Although this may seem hard, it is essential that your older dog doesn't feel the need to compete with the puppy as this can lead to conflict between them.

If a placid older dog allows the puppy to jump all over him and doesn't gently tell him off, the puppy may learn that this is acceptable behaviour. If he tries the same thing with a strange dog in the park, the puppy will probably be strongly reprimanded – and this can set up a fear of unknown dogs, which can later lead to aggression towards them.

To avoid this, follow the rules below:

Allow your older dog to tell your puppy off if he's being too rough. This should not involve any physical harm to your puppy, but should teach him or her to be more respectful.

Give your older dog time with you, away from the pup.

Keep all play between your older dog and pup controlled and supervised. Intervene and have 'time out' if it becomes too rough – especially if your older dog is very placid and will allow the puppy to bully.

Take your puppy out without your older dog at least as much as they go out together. Some puppies learn to rely on their older 'friends' for support and cannot cope without them.

TRAINING EXERCISE 2

What's my name?

This is probably *the* most important bit of early training: if you can get your dog to look at you the instant you say his name, wherever you happen to be and whatever distractions are present, the rest of his training is likely to be relatively easy.

1

Start in a distraction-free area. Hold a food treat between your thumb and finger and, as soon as your dog sniffs at it, lift your hand so that it is between your eyes.

TOP TIP

ALWAYS CLICK OR SAY 'GOOD' WHEN HE LOOKS AT YOU IN RESPONSE AND GIVE A TREAT OR A GAME. DOGS QUICKLY LEARN TO IGNORE THEIR OWNERS IF THEY SIMPLY REPEAT THEIR NAMES AND FAIL TO GIVE THEM REWARDS.

2

Click or say 'Good' and immediately reward him for looking towards your face. Repeat this four times.

3

On the fifth go, say your dog's name in a cheerful voice. Keep your hand still by your side. If he looks at your face, click or say 'Good' and then give him a tasty reward. If he is reluctant, then bring your hand towards your face to help him.

4

Repeat this pattern four or five times, rewarding when your dog looks at your face.

5

Now, without any food in your hand, ask your dog for his attention by saying his name. The instant he looks up at your face, you can click and reward him generously. Repeat this action until it's perfect.

TRAINING EXERCISE 3

Come when called

It's essential for basic safety that your dog is trained to come straight to you every time you call him.

1

Standing or crouching only a couple of steps away from your dog, call him in a friendly voice.

TOP TIP

NEVER CALL YOUR DOG TO YOU AND THEN DO SOMETHING UNPLEASANT, SUCH AS FLEA SPRAYING OR GIVING MEDICAL TREATMENTS. HE'S LIKELY TO VIEW THIS AS A PUNISHMENT FOR COMING WHEN CALLED.

2

Waggle a tasty food lure in your outstretched hand and then start moving backwards.

3

If he shows no response, clap your hands or make silly noises until he comes towards you. The instant that he does so, click or say 'Good' and then give him several treats straight away, putting them on the floor in front of you.

4

Gradually increase the distance he has to come to get the food, making sure you praise and reward him for coming when you call him.

5

Now practise calling your dog to you at unusual moments in and around the house, and then outside in the garden or yard. Build up his recall before you practise in the park or woods where there are distractions.

PUPPY SMART

(INTELLIGENCE)

People often ask which is the most intelligent breed or type of dog, but this is not easy to quantify as dogs are often 'experts' in their own behavioural niche — such as searching for things by scent, or picking up training commands or visual cues. Other dogs learn quickly how to please themselves — by running off rather than coming back when called or stealing items in the home and chewing them up — and although we might be tempted to call this naughty or annoying, it's certainly very clever!

All puppies need to spend a lot of time exploring, experimenting and discovering the world around them. This builds neural networks in the brain and improves their problem-solving abilities and coping mechanisms. This is another reason why getting a puppy from an enriched home environment is so important, as dogs raised in deprived circumstances can be adversely affected for life.

MEET

Mattie, the Dalmatian

Her distinctive spots and bold features make Mattie an eye-catching pup. As well as pulling up grass and digging holes in the ground, she loves to play catch. She is lively and energetic but is also very observant and thoughtful, and can be found watching wildlife documentaries on the television. Her mischievous puppy side is still present though, and she has been known to untie the shoes of the person walking her when out and about! She's a growing puppy and whenever she gets hungry she will pick up her bowl and carry it around her home until she's fed.

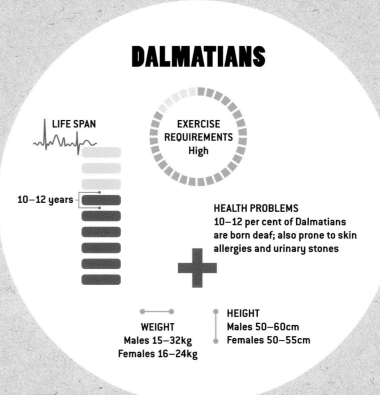

DALMATIANS

LIFE SPAN

10–12 years

EXERCISE REQUIREMENTS
High

HEALTH PROBLEMS
10–12 per cent of Dalmatians are born deaf; also prone to skin allergies and urinary stones

WEIGHT
Males 15–32kg
Females 16–24kg

HEIGHT
Males 50–60cm
Females 50–55cm

TERRIBLE TWOS

13–16 weeks

THE JUVENILE PERIOD

At this stage in their life, puppies are classed as being in their juvenile period. The rate at which they develop depends to a large extent on the breed: small, fast-maturing breeds, such as some of the smaller terriers, may well have acquired most of their adult behaviours and physical attributes by the time they are 16 weeks, while slow-maturing breeds such as Newfoundlands may still look and behave like immature puppies at the same age.

Some distinctive 'breed features' – both physical and behavioural – also become more apparent. For example, many puppies – such as German Shepherds – are born with floppy ears, and it is often only in this phase that their ears are finally fully erect. In other types, such as Cocker Spaniels, the wispy fluff of the puppy coat starts to be replaced by a 'saddle' of coarser hair, which first appears on the dog's back. Retrievers of all kinds will want to pick things up and carry them, while herding types may start to stalk and pounce on each other!

Puppies of this age seem to have a boundless supply of energy! You might be tempted to try and wear your puppy out by giving him lots of exercise, but remember that he is still growing: limbs are not at their final length and joints and muscles are not fully formed, leaving them vulnerable to over-exercise and the damage that this can do.

STOPPING YOUR PUPPY FROM CHEWING THINGS

Give your dog plenty of safe chew toys! Toys that reward the dog for chewing them are ideal. Kongs stuffed with food are designed specially so that small pieces of food come out while the dog is chewing.

All dogs need to chew – especially around teething time when their gums may be inflamed. Sadly, dogs do not know the difference between a stick and a table leg, nor an old slipper and a brand new trainer.

A small number of puppies may also chew to relieve boredom, frustration or distress when left alone at home. Make sure you leave him for only short periods of time and give him wonderfully rewarding toys to chew and play with that he never has at any other time.

If your dog is chewing and ingesting inappropriate items, remove these items and replace with a safe chew toy.

Also at this time, the puppy's deciduous teeth start to be replaced by adult ones and this, combined with the dog's natural curiosity, means that they need to chew – a lot! Most will pick up and chew almost anything, including your furniture and shoes, so make sure you provide plenty of safe chew toys.

Puppies need to see, hear and smell all the many aspects of the world around them, and learn how to respond or ignore all these stimuli if they are to become a well-balanced adult dog. If you're worried about vaccinations not being complete (which is usually at around 12 weeks of age; see page 60), carry your puppy and allow him to interact with other dogs that you know have been fully vaccinated.

Behaviourists sometimes call the period between 13 and 16 weeks the 'Age of Cutting' – cutting both teeth and apron strings! Many owners find that their puppy begins to test social boundaries, almost like a stroppy teenager – by refusing to come when called or comply with requests and finding out what works and what doesn't – and 'temper tantrums', such as struggling when gently restrained, are common. Keep calm and set clear boundaries so that the pup knows where he stands and what behaviour is acceptable to you; you'll have fewer battles later on!

THE 'FEAR PERIOD'

Many puppies go through a 'fear period' at around this time, showing fear of objects or events that they were completely comfortable with only the day or week before. This can be explained by looking at the dog's wild ancestry. In a wild dog pack, a litter of puppies would stay close to the den site with at least one or two adults to keep them safe, even if the rest of the pack was away hunting. Suddenly, domestic puppies are much more mobile at this stage; they may even wander off by themselves to explore or play. Becoming fearful of new stimuli or experiences therefore keeps them safe, as they are more likely to run away from something they have never met before than to approach it.

While this is perfectly normal, you need to handle it in the right way if the pup's fear is not to become established. If your puppy shows fear of any new or even familiar person, dog or event, try to ignore the behaviour as much as possible, and praise and reward brave behaviour instead.

GETTING YOUR PUPPY NEUTERED

Neutering can have really great health benefits for your dog – and you'll also be doing your bit to help prevent pets being abandoned or even put to sleep because there aren't enough homes to go around.

With castration both testicles are removed, which takes away the main source of the male hormone testosterone. Male dogs can be castrated from 12 weeks onwards, but on the whole, dogs need to mature before being castrated, and the ideal time seems to be between eight months and a year. Some conditions, such as testicular cancer, can be prevented if neutering is done before middle age. However, castrating dogs whose behaviours are testosterone driven will not, as is often assumed, 'calm him down'.

Female dogs can be spayed from around five months, but veterinary opinion differs on whether they should have a season first. Spaying is effective in preventing mammary tumours and a serious womb infection called pyometra. Urinary incontinence may be seen in bitches spayed at any age, but seems more prevalent in those that are allowed to become overweight and are spayed before their first season.

TOP TIP

SEVERAL CHARITIES, INCLUDING THE BLUE CROSS, THE DOGS TRUST AND THE RSPCA, CAN HELP WITH THE COST OF NEUTERING DOGS, SO CONTACT YOUR NEAREST ONE TO FIND OUT MORE.

PUPPY SUPER POWERS

(SENSES AND PUPPIES WITH SPECIAL SKILLS)

Selective breeding has meant that individual breeds and types are especially good at certain behaviours and skills, and these are often used to help us in work or sport.

Although all healthy dogs rely on a range of senses to explore and interact with us and the world around them, many have finely honed sets of sensory skills which set them apart as 'experts' in their field.

BLOODHOUND

This dog is renowned for its incredible tracking abilities — and even has ears that have developed to hang down when the dog is following a trail and waft scent molecules towards the dog's nose.

SIBERIAN HUSKY

Built to run, but at a pace and speed that is incredibly efficient, making this a long-distance runner to be envied. These dogs can even go to the toilet on the move!

NEWFOUNDLAND

Excellent swimmers, these dogs were bred to help fishermen bring in the nets in the icy waters of the east coast of Canada. They have webbed feet and huge, thick coats to protect them from the cold.

BASENJI

This unusual breed, reputed to be the pets of the Pharaohs, was originally used for hunting outdoors, and cleaning up the children's nappies indoors! It has no bark, but expresses itself through a unique 'yodel' instead.

TRAINING EXERCISE 4

Sit!

There are at least 101 things that your dog cannot do if he's sitting, so it's an essential skill for him to learn!

1

Show your dog a food treat. Hold it tightly between your finger and thumb, so that he can smell it and even taste it but can't steal it from you.

2

Position the treat close to his nose. Slowly lift your hand up and back, so that he has to look right up in order to follow your fingers.

3

This causes a physical chain reaction – as he raises his head, his rear end has to go down. The instant his bottom hits the ground, click or say 'Good' and give him the treat. Repeat this action at least five times.

4

Now repeat the movement again, but this time say the word 'Sit' just before you move the food lure.

WITHOUT THE LURE

1

Keep your hand in exactly the same position as previously, but this time don't hold any food in it.

2

Ask your dog to sit. If he does so, click or say 'Good' immediately, then give him a food treat from your other hand, or from a pot or pouch.

TOP TIP

ONCE YOUR DOG HAS GOT THE HANG OF MOVING INTO THE RIGHT POSITION, STOP USING THE LURE AS QUICKLY AS POSSIBLE TO PREVENT RELIANCE ON THE FOOD.

SEPARATION ANXIETY

Dogs are social animals, who need company and may suffer if left alone with nothing to do for long periods of time. There is a risk that your puppy may become over-dependent on one or more members of your household, leading to what is known as 'separation anxiety' – being unable to cope without his owner being present. Dogs with separation problems may howl, whine or bark when left. They may lose control of their bowel or bladder and may mess indoors, or they may become destructive, chewing, scratching or shedding items, door frames or furnishings in an attempt to follow their owner. To avoid this, teach your puppy to be left alone for short periods. Here are some useful tips:

🐾 Do not allow your puppy to be your 'shadow' when you are at home. Shut doors between you regularly and routinely, so that your puppy cannot always have contact with you.

🐾 Give attention when you choose rather than always when your pup demands it.

🐾 Make sure your puppy is tired and has been to the toilet before you leave him on his own.

🐾 Feeding your puppy will make him more sleepy and restful.

🐾 Leave your puppy with the radio on and a really enjoyable chew toy. A Kong stuffed with food or a chewy bone is ideal.

🐾 Leave quickly and quietly. Do not fuss your pup before leaving.

🐾 Leave your pup for only a few minutes to begin with, then build up the time to an hour or so.

🐾 On your return, be matter of fact. Take your puppy into the garden to relieve himself straight away. Do not scold him for going to the toilet indoors in your absence.

🐾 Practise leaving your pup by himself little and often. 2 hours is the suggested time that puppies can be left under the age of 5 months.

TRAINING EXERCISE 5

Down!

Teaching your dog to lie down needs a little more patience than the sit position (page 88), but be persistent.

(page 88)

1

With your dog sitting, hold a food lure close to his nose. Lower your hand very slowly to the floor, directly between his front paws. Hang on to the treat by turning your palm down, with the food hidden inside your hand.

2

You will soon be able to tell if your dog is trying if his front end goes down in a bowing position, or if he moves backwards slightly. Both these things mean you just have to wait. Don't be tempted to move your hand along the floor, as this will lure the dog back into a standing position.

3

Be patient – if your dog loses interest, just show him the treat and then lure him towards the floor, before turning your hand palm down, so that the treat is hidden.

4

The instant your dog lies down, click and then drop the treat on to the floor between his front paws and let him eat it. (This prevents him from following your hand back up again like a yo-yo.)

5

Repeat several times, sometimes with the food in your hand, sometimes without. Still click and put a treat on the floor after your dog has moved into the down position. Once you can guarantee he will lie down by following your hand to the floor, say the word 'Down' just before moving the lure.

STAY DOWN

Once your dog has learned to lie down on command, you can teach him to stay in that position for longer, by waiting before you click and treat. Build this up from just five seconds to 90 seconds, over several training sessions.

GROOMING

Many owners automatically imagine that only long-coated breeds need substantial amounts of grooming. However, even the smoothest-coated dog will need to have his or her ears cleaned, teeth brushed, and coat bathed from time to time.

Ears

Inspect a pup's ears by lifting the ear flap and wipe the flap and visible parts with dampened cotton wool if necessary. Never poke anything such as cotton buds into the ear. Seek veterinary advice immediately if you find a brown discharge or the ear canal smells offensive.

Teeth & mouth

At least once a week, put a little specially designed dog toothpaste on one finger or a finger brush and rub gently on the teeth and gums, working from front to back, sweeping the brush from the gum down the tooth to dislodge food particles and to gently massage the gums.

Eyes

In some breeds or individuals, the eyes weep a little and leave a brown discharge. Wipe the tear patches with dampened cotton wool, but avoid any ointments, drops or other substances near the dog's eyes unless prescribed by a vet.

Brushing & combing

Choose a soft, gentle brush to start with; rubber ones are ideal, as they massage the skin rather than pull through the hair. Use a comb for feathering and fine hair around the face and ears, being careful not to pull or tug at any knots beneath the surface; it's better to cut these out.

Bathing

Most dogs only need to be bathed around twice a year if they are groomed regularly and are not prone to rolling in offensive odours! Bathing too frequently strips the coat of natural oils and waterproofing. Make sure that the water is warm, but not hot, and rinse all shampoo out of the coat thoroughly. Dry and brush your pup afterwards and keep him warm; it's easy for damp dogs to become chilled.

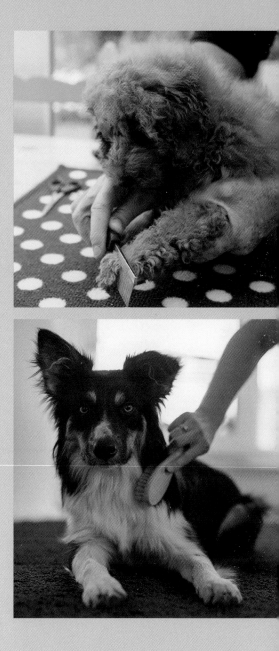

MEET

Coral, the Cocker Spaniel

Coral is a beloved companion with a cheerful personality. She is playful, attentive and energetic and she enjoys any form of exercise. Coral loves to play catch with her favourite toy, which she plays tug with anyone willing to play along. She has already learnt to sit on command and loves homemade treats. Coral has quite a sensitive nature too, and enjoys spending quality time with her family on the sofa.

COCKER SPANIELS

LIFE SPAN

11–12 years

EXERCISE REQUIREMENTS
High

HEALTH PROBLEMS
Prone to cancer and benign tumours, also cataracts

WEIGHT
Males 13–16kg
Females 12–15kg

HEIGHT
Males 39–41cm
Females 36–38cm

TRAINING YOUR DOG

4–6 months

PRE-ADOLESCENCE

In physical terms, the most notable feature of this stage of a puppy's life is that the 'puppy' teeth are replaced by permanent, adult ones.

Puppy teeth are very sharp! They are typically narrower than adult teeth and are less robust — which makes sense, as it's not until they hit this juvenile stage that puppies need teeth that are able to withstand more wear and tear.

Most puppies have 28 puppy teeth in total — they lack molars (as they do not need to crush bones in food at this stage). The puppy teeth are replaced by 42 adult teeth over a number of weeks. Puppies lose their teeth in a strict order, but not necessarily to a strict time scale. Most start to lose their tiny incisors (the teeth right at the front between the 'fangs') at around 12 weeks, but this can occur earlier or later depending on the individual. The other teeth then quickly follow, and the puppy will have a complete set of adult teeth by the time he is 22 weeks.

STOPPING YOUR PUPPY FROM DIGGING

Digging is work for idle paws, and most dogs only dig because they are bored. If you want to stop your dog from digging in your garden or landscaping your lawn, there are a few basic rules that you must understand:

Some breeds – terriers, in particular – need to dig as part of their natural behaviour. It's what they were bred to do.

If you intend to leave your dog outside without supervision, you must give him things to keep him occupied.

Telling dogs off for digging will not stop the behaviour – in fact, it often makes it worse as they get attention from their owners for doing the 'wrong' thing.

You can channel your dog's natural digging instincts into a more acceptable behaviour by giving him his own place to dig.

Choose an area for your dog to dig in. This could be part of a flower bed or a child's sandpit. Fill it with loose sand.

Take your dog to this area every day and let him watch while you hide goodies such as bones, chews or toys in there.

Allow him to dig in this area.

TOP TIP

TOO WET OUTDOORS? CREATE A 'DIGGING BOX' INDOORS USING A CARDBOARD BOX AND LAYERS OF OLD TOWELS WITH TREATS AND TOYS HIDDEN BETWEEN.

Just as in children, you may find a 'baby' tooth that has fallen out – but it will be just the hollow top of the tooth, with no root attached. This is because the pressure of the new tooth bud forming directly beneath the puppy tooth causes the root to be reabsorbed into the system, which then allows the new adult tooth to grow down in its place.

Sometimes, some baby teeth are retained. This mostly affects the canine teeth and occurs when the permanent tooth bud does not grow immediately under the puppy tooth, meaning that the adult tooth appears right next to it instead, so the pup has two 'fangs' on each side. Surgery to remove the baby tooth may be necessary if problems occur.

Adult teeth may be less sharp than puppy teeth, but they are well designed for tearing, shearing and crushing. Adult teeth may take several weeks to fully appear, and some breeds or individuals may never develop a full set; tiny breeds seem particularly prone to having missing dentition.

Just like us, dogs' teeth need brushing every day if they are to stay in good condition (see page 94).

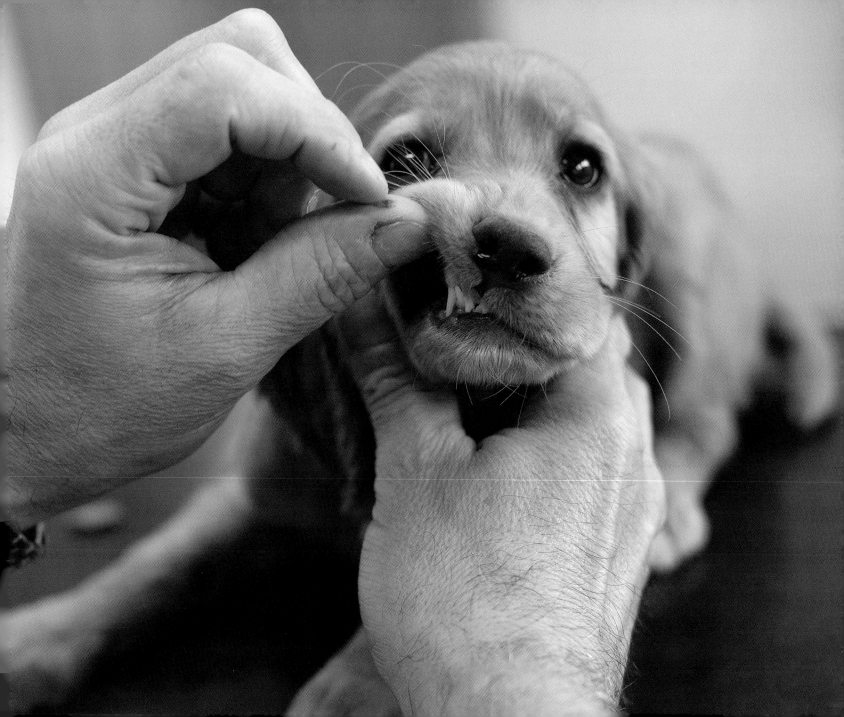

TRAINING EXERCISE 6

Walking on the lead – stage 1

It may seem rather odd, but the best way to train your dog to walk nicely on the lead is to start by standing still. This is because taking even one single step in the direction that the dog wants to go will reward him for pulling.

1

Start off by putting your dog on the lead in the sitting room, kitchen, hallway or garden. Stand still. Hold the lead close to your body to prevent your hand from being pulled towards him.

2

Hold a tasty food treat in the hand closest to your dog and let him know it's there. As soon as he puts slack in the lead and looks at you, click or say 'Good', and then give him the treat by dropping it close to your heel. Dropping the treat on the floor prevents snatching, and also encourages your dog to focus on the floor, rather than on your hands.

3

Turn slightly on the spot, so that your body moves a little but your feet stay still. Your dog will have to take a step or two to keep next to your side. Watch his position — if there is any tension in the lead, stand still and wait, making sure the hand holding the lead stays in place.

4

Every time there's some slack in the lead, just click or say 'Good' and give your dog a food treat to reward him for his behaviour. Do this by placing it beside your heel.

5

Repeat this exercise several times and then stop and have an enjoyable game together.

TRAINING EXERCISE 7

Walking on the lead – stage 2

Once your dog has started to understand that slack in the lead will lead to a reward, the next stage is to get him to comply when you are both moving.

1

As in stage 1 (see page 104), start off by standing still, with your dog on the lead standing beside you.

2

Keep your dog's attention, and take one or two steps. Click when you see a 'J' in the lead, and then drop the food treat for him to eat.

3

Set off again – this time three steps – always watching for the slack lead that gets rewards and standing still as soon as there is any tension.

4

Repeat this exercise several times, taking just a few steps at a time and clicking and giving your dog treats for a slack lead. Once your dog has mastered this, you can move on to walking for a few paces and then changing direction, using the same 'click and reward' system as before.

TOP TIP

AT THIS STAGE, SOME DOGS TRY TO USE THEIR STRENGTH, BODY WEIGHT, OR LOW CENTRE OF GRAVITY TO PULL YOU OFF BALANCE. KEEP THE HAND HOLDING THE LEAD TUCKED INTO YOUR WAISTBAND TO PREVENT THIS.

CLIPPING YOUR DOG'S TOENAILS

Nearly all dogs need their toenails clipping about every three to four weeks. Training your pup to stand still and allow you to lift his feet will make the process much less stressful for both of you. Cut your dog's claws little and often. Frequently clipping the nails encourages the quick to recede away from the end of the nail, making it less likely that you'll catch it accidentally.

1

Leave the clippers in the cupboard! Pick up each foot in turn, then give a food treat. Repeat this several times a day for at least three or four days.

2

Pick up each foot in turn and this time hold it firmly, while extending one claw so that you can inspect it for at least five seconds. Do this for each claw on each foot, giving the dog a food treat for calm behaviour. Repeat this frequently over three or four days.

3

Now get the clippers out, but do not try to cut any claws! Show the dog the clippers and give him a treat. Do this several times until he really looks forward to seeing those clippers.

4

Hold each foot in turn and extend a claw. Tap the clippers on the claw lightly, then give the dog a treat. Do not cut the claw. Do this for each nail on each foot and repeat it until your puppy is calm and confident with the procedure.

5

You are now ready to cut the claws — but cut no more than 1mm off the end of each nail, as the blood supply to the nail (the quick) runs the length of the nail and ends quite close to the surface. If accidentally cut, this can be very painful and will bleed profusely. You can always cut more off later. Give a special reward for good behaviour of several treats and a good game.

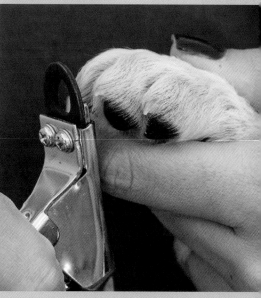

GROWING PUP

As puppies grow, visible signs of their developing co-ordination are more than apparent. Once wobbly puppies become adept at climbing, jumping, running and pouncing on toys and their litter mates. This can lead to anxious times for breeders and owners, as it's a fine balance between allowing a pup the freedom to explore and build muscle to support joints and bones, and the risks of over-exercise or injury.

It's a sad fact
that nearly half of all pet dogs
are thought to be overweight — and
obesity in puppyhood can lead to weight
problems in adult dogs. However, like all
fitness and exercise regimes, we need
to ensure we start slowly and build up
gradually to avoid strain on the
body and young joints
and bones.

On the whole, the rule
'little and often' is a good one
to follow when considering how much
exercise your pup should have. Puppies need
spurts of activity and gentle exercise, which
can be gradually built up over time to increase
fitness and strength, interspersed with rest
and sleep — during which time pups
build brain power via increased
neural networks.

DEALING WITH FLEAS

It's every dog owner's nightmare — your pet pooch constantly scratching bites from tiny fleas that can barely be seen with the naked eye. And it's painful and potentially dangerous, too. If a dog becomes allergic to the fleas' saliva, scabby and infected lesions may develop all over the body, particularly along the back and the back of the thighs. In a small puppy, a heavy infestation can cause clinical anaemia and associated weakness, as the fleas feed on the puppy's blood.

It's usually fairly obvious if your puppy has fleas, but here are the tell-tale signs:

Is your pet scratching?

Can you see tiny, dark specks in its fur, or small, browny-black insects?

Do you have any unaccounted-for insect bites yourself?

If the answer to these questions is yes, then you must treat the infestation as soon as possible; in the warm and dry environment of your house, the adult fleas will quickly start to lay eggs that, within as little as 12 days, may develop into new adults also capable of breeding. Consult your vet for a suitable prescription treatment.

In addition to treating your pup, however, you should also treat the house with a long-acting insecticidal spray. Wash your puppy's bedding every week. Vacuum furniture, floors and skirting boards two or three times a week to help destroy fleas. Also throw away the dustbag from your hoover after each vacuuming.

DID YOU KNOW...?

Your dog can become infested with tapeworms via ingesting an infected flea: yet another reason to ensure your pup is flea-free.

FLEA FACTS

Some types of flea can leap more than 100 times their own body length.

It's estimated that 95 per cent of flea eggs, larvae and pupae live in the environment, not on your pet.

Fleas can lie dormant in your carpet or furnishings. Undisturbed and without a blood meal, a flea can live more than 100 days.

A female flea can lay up to 50 eggs in one day — that's 2,000 eggs in her lifetime.

A female flea consumes 15 times her own body weight in blood daily.

Female fleas begin to lay eggs within 36–48 hours of their first blood meal.

MEET

Ruby, the Toy Poodle

Ruby is a ball of energy. She loves to bound around the garden and her incredibly curious side means she's always alert to any interesting sniff or sound. She is very friendly to anything she meets, be it animal or human, however, she does enjoy chasing after the pigeons in the garden. Exhausted after all that running about, she loves to nap in her favourite sunny spot – the conservatory window seat. She was hesitant the first time she was groomed, but soon got used to it and now cannot wait until the next time.

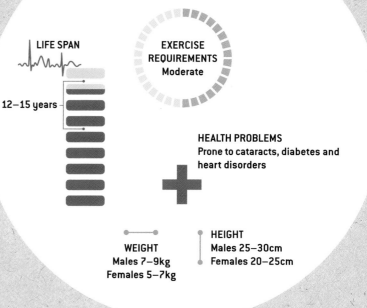

TOY POODLES

LIFE SPAN

12–15 years

EXERCISE REQUIREMENTS
Moderate

HEALTH PROBLEMS
Prone to cataracts, diabetes and heart disorders

WEIGHT
Males 7–9kg
Females 5–7kg

HEIGHT
Males 25–30cm
Females 20–25cm

THE TEENAGE STAGE

6–12 months

ADOLESCENCE

Six to twelve months of age could easily be called the 'teenage' stage of a pup's development. Puppies of between six and nine months are often rather awkward, gangly and clumsy in appearance. They may also attempt to behave as if they are adult dogs, while still appearing very puppy-like in movement and posture. The puppy will need less frequent meals, cutting back from four or five meals a day at 12 weeks to only two at six months old.

Many 'teenage' dogs can be quite exasperating! Males, in particular, can be driven by the hormone testosterone and behave in an excessively sexual, competitive or even aggressive manner, particularly towards other dogs. Neutering (see page 85) may well be a good option for such dogs, but training is always needed, too.

Teeth are fully adult now, and are well set into the jaw bone. Chewing is still a necessity and nearly all dogs, no matter what their age, continue to enjoy chewing on a bone or toy.

Dogs usually grow their 'adult' coat by the time they are seven or eight months of age. This is normally harsher and longer than the fluffy puppy coat, and typically starts as a 'saddle' effect on the back, depending on the dog's breed and coat type. However, the full adult coat usually takes up to a year to grow, and this may affect the dog's eventual colouring.

Male dogs may begin to lift their legs to urinate during this period and females may come into season for the first time. In some bitches this can be as early as seven months; in others it may not occur until as late as 14 months. Domestic dogs commonly have two seasons per year. For most bitches, their first season is a little bewildering. Hormonal changes may affect her mood, and other dogs may start to pester her as she begins to smell more attractive. There are several signs that your bitch may be coming into season: she may lick herself more, and you may notice that her vulva is slightly swollen. Many bitches also urinate more frequently before they come into season, often in tiny amounts over a wide area.

By the age of one year, it is possible for a dog to have increased his or her birth weight by at least 60 times! These are now the months of maturity. Most dogs will have reached their full height by this point, but they still have much more 'filling out' to do. In males, particularly, the chest is likely to deepen after this time, and the head is likely to broaden a little, depending on the breed. Dogs will easily have attained their adult strength by this stage, and they will be able to control their bodies fully.

DID YOU KNOW…?

By seven months of age, a puppy may have increased his or her birth weight by 15–40 times, depending on the breed.

STOPPING YOUR PUPPY FROM JUMPING UP

Dogs jump up to be friendly! As very young puppies, they solicit attention from their mother by licking and nuzzling at her mouth. Later, this becomes a greeting gesture that is used amongst dogs. In order to reach our faces, of course, dogs have to jump up!

Thankfully, teaching 'sit to greet' is relatively simple. First, make sure that all jumping up of any kind at home is ignored. Turn your back and fold your arms if the puppy jumps up; praise and pet him if he is sitting or being calm.

Then, ask a friend to help. Have your puppy on the lead. When your friend arrives, ask them to ignore your puppy completely to begin with. When your puppy tires of bouncing and sits or lies down, click, praise and give a food treat. Your friend can then praise and pet your puppy, but must instantly stand up and turn away again if he jumps up.

In the UK, it is now a legal requirement for all dogs over the age of eight weeks to be tagged with a microchip. The microchip itself is about the same size as a grain of rice. It carries information about the dog in the form of a unique serial number, which can then be fed into a computer to trace the keeper's details so that, if your dog goes missing, you can be quickly reunited.

The information stored on the chip is held by one of a number of approved databases. Which one it is held on will be determined by the veterinary practice or welfare centre that supplied the chip – and it's important that, as a new owner, you know which one your pet is registered with as you will need to make sure that you have changed the 'keepership' details with the database.

DID YOU KNOW...?

It's a legal requirement for your dog to wear a collar or harness with a visible ID tag when in public. This is a low-tech but effective way of making sure your pet is safe.

Training an adolescent dog

Unfortunately, this is also the time when training seems to have been forgotten and encouraging your exuberant, adolescent dog to come back when it is called in the park or garden can be a long and arduous process! Much more time and effort is required in training an adolescent dog than is needed in training a puppy.

Dogs are generally calmer once they get to 18 months or so, especially as they have built relationships within the family and understand the daily routine. However, it's perhaps not surprising that many dogs end up in rescue shelters between the ages of seven and 18 months. Having not had adequate training and socialisation in the early weeks, they do not know how to behave in a calm and sensible manner around humans or other dogs.

By the age of one, your dog's character will be fully formed; although he will continue to learn throughout his life, his personality and general outlook are here to stay. Attitudes formed as a puppy often have far-reaching effects, and owners are often disappointed that their dog has not 'grown out' of certain behaviours that they do not like. This does not mean that re-training is not possible after the puppy stage – but it can be much harder. Just as it is much easier for us to learn a foreign language at five years of age than 55, so dogs will need more time and patience committed to re-training or rehabilitation after this time.

PUPPY VERSUS WORLD

(INDEPENDENCE)

Pups vary greatly in social confidence: even in the same litter, some are brazen and extrovert while others are shy and worried, and there's little doubt that this is due to a combination of inherited genetics, their mother's behaviour, and how they are raised.

For the vast majority, pups develop more and more coping strategies as time goes on and gradually begin to show signs of developing independence as they head into the juvenile stage.

Puppies are absorbing information every minute that they are awake, and much of their learning is about what feels good and what doesn't. Just like us, they need to discover that the world is potentially full of new experiences and encounters — and that these can be good, bad or indifferent. It's how they are handled that matters!

Given reassurance, guidance and lots of opportunities for socialisation, pups soon learn to conquer their fear of unknown dogs, noises and sights in the big, wide world, and start to show signs of real independence. This might manifest itself in tackling the stairs, dipping a paw into the sea at the beach, running off with another dog's ball at the park, or barking at next door's cat.

TRAINING EXERCISE 8

Stand!

Teaching a stand can be very useful, especially for visits to the vet and when grooming your dog. It also means that you can dry his feet easily with a towel without having a battle.

1

With your dog in a sit position, hold a food treat right in front of his nose. Now move your hand away slowly, parallel to the floor, at his head height.

2

As soon as your dog moves forwards into a stand position, click or say 'Good' and give him the treat.

3

Practise this exercise until your dog is confident in just following your hand without the treat in it.

4

At this stage you can add the cue word 'Stand' just before he moves into position.

TOP TIP

IF YOUR DOG LIES DOWN, YOUR HAND IS TOO LOW. IF HE JUMPS UP, IT IS PROBABLY TOO HIGH. IF HE WALKS MORE THAN ONE STEP FORWARD, YOU ARE MOVING THE TREAT TOO FAR AND TOO FAST.

YOUR DOG'S AGE IN HUMAN YEARS

We've all heard the saying that one year of a dog's life is equivalent to seven years for a human, but things are not as clear cut as that — different breeds and sizes of dog age at different rates. A more accurate way of comparing the 'human age' of your dog is to use its weight as a guide.

YOUR DOG'S AGE	YOUR DOG'S WEIGHT				
	7–13kg	14–22kg	23–34kg	35–45kg	46kg+
1	12	13	15	17	20
2	19	19	21	23	26
3	25	25	27	29	32
4	30	31	32	34	37
5	35	36	37	39	42
6	40	40	42	44	47
7	44	45	46	49	52
8	48	49	51	53	57
9	52	53	55	57	62
10	55	56	59	62	67
11	59	60	63	66	72
12	62	64	67	71	77
13	66	67	71	76	83
14	69	71	76	81	90
15	73	75	80	86	96
16	77	80	85	92	104
17	82	84	91	99	112
18	86	89	97	106	121
19	91	95	103	114	131
20	97	101	111	122	142

BARKING

Dogs bark for a number of different reasons: to raise the alarm about intruders, to show distress or fear, to keep away animals or people that they feel threatened by, or to seek attention or try to call their owners when they have been left alone. So what can you do if your pup barks a lot of the time?

First, ask yourself why your puppy may be doing this. If he is barking at other dogs, is there fear involved or is it sheer excitement? More socialisation may be required to get him used to other dogs, or you may need to train him to 'shush' on command.

DID YOU KNOW...?

An adult dog's bark is an acoustic mix of a warning sound and a puppy distress cry.

If your puppy is barking for your attention, show him this behaviour is unacceptable by consistently getting up and leaving the room, turning your back on him, or putting him in another room for a few minutes. Giving eye contact, shouting or telling your puppy off are all likely to make matters worse — you're rewarding him by giving him attention, and he even may think you're joining in!

TRAINING EXERCISE 9

Leave it!

Dogs explore the world by picking things up with their mouths to check how they taste and feel. They also steal items for attention. Teaching your dog not to touch things can be a real life-saver, as well as saving your sanity.

1

Hold a tasty treat in your hand, and close your fingers around it tightly. Present your hand to your dog and wait patiently while he sniffs, licks and nibbles, trying to get the food.

2

Keep your hand still — do not be tempted to pull it away from your dog. Stay quiet — it's important that you do not say anything.

3

Watch carefully. As soon as your dog takes his nose away from your hand, even for a split second, click, or say 'Good', then release the treat.

4

Repeat this several times, clicking and giving a treat every time you see daylight between your dog's muzzle and your hand. Most dogs learn this incredibly quickly — usually in four to six repetitions.

5

Now wait until your dog has taken his nose away from your hand for the count of three, then click and treat. At this stage, lots of dogs will turn their face away as if to resist temptation. If you see this happening, click and treat immediately.

MOVING ON TO AN OPEN HAND

The next stage is to take the training further, so you are using an open hand, and then to add a cue. Here's how you do it.

1

With the food still closed in your hand, build up the amount of time that your dog will wait with his nose well away from your hand to about ten seconds. Keep on practising until this is perfect, and at least four times.

2

At this point you can add in the command 'Leave'. Say this in a calm, quiet voice, not a threatening one. You need to say the word before you move your hand down to your dog's eye level.

3

Once your dog has got the hang of this, repeat the exercise, but this time say 'Leave', and then present the food on your open hand.

4

If your dog tries to take the food from your open palm, simply close your fingers around it again. Do not jerk your hand away. This is very important, as it is likely to encourage some dogs to snatch.

5

Click and treat your dog for moving away from the food, as you did before, even though he can see it.

6

Gradually build up the time that your dog keeps his nose away from the food once you have given him the command to leave. See if you can get him to wait for ten seconds before you click and reward.

MEET

Dakin, the Golden Retriever

Adventurous, lively and confident, Dakin is a bundle of energy and a little hooligan — when he wants to be! He can often be found following his nose around the garden with his favourite toy Moose affectionately lodged between his teeth. Dakin enjoys chewing plastic cartons and eating small treats of strong mature cheddar cheese. He's not sure about motorbikes and gets a fright when he sees his own reflection in the car window.

GOLDEN RETRIEVERS

LIFE SPAN

10–12 years

EXERCISE REQUIREMENTS
High

HEALTH PROBLEMS
Prone to hip and elbow dysplasia and eye problems

WEIGHT
Males 29–34kg
Females 25–29kg

HEIGHT
Males 56–61cm
Females 51–56cm

A DAY IN THE LIFE OF A PUPPY

ON THEIR WALK PUPPIES LIKE TO...

MORNING

TOILET

BREAKFAST

It's best to feed your dog the same food as the breeder used. Puppies need to be fed little and often.

WALKS

Puppies need exercise but don't over do it as their bones are still developing. Best to carry them outside and walk with them a little.

TRAINING

Start training your puppy by familiarising it with their name. Or getting them used to the instruction 'sit'.

NAP

LUNCH

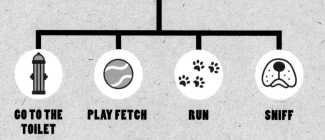

GO TO THE TOILET   **PLAY FETCH**   **RUN**   **SNIFF**

TOILET   **ACTIVITY**   **NAP**   **HOME TIME**   **DINNER**   **TOILET**   **SLEEP**

ACTIVITY
Start socialising your puppy with other dogs but only if they have been fully vaccinated.

HOME TIME
If people come home after work or school try to keep things calm and practice training.

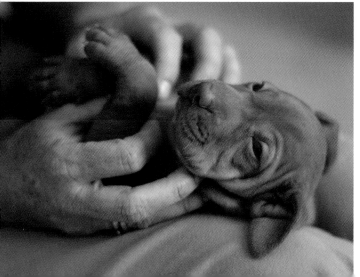

RESOURCES

USEFUL WEBSITES

Association of Pet Dog Trainers (UK)
www.apdt.co.uk

All About Dog Food
www.allaboutdogfood.co.uk

Clever Dog Company
www.cleverdogcompany.com

Clickertraining.com
www.clickertraining.com

Dogmantics
www.dogmantics.com

Dog Star Daily
www.dogstardaily.com

Fast Results Dog Training
www.21daystoacleverdog.com

Help with Behaviour Problems
www.apbc.org.uk

Learn to Talk Dog
www.learntotalkdog.com

The Bark
http://thebark.com/content/
breeds-and-behavior

The Kennel Club
www.thekennelclub.org.uk

Train your dog online
www.trainyourdogonline.com

Welfare in Dog Training
http://www.dogwelfarecampaign.org/
why-not-dominance.php

FURTHER READING

Brain Games for Dogs, Claire Arrowsmith

Clever Dog, Sarah Whitehead

Complete Puppy and Dog Care, Bruce Fogle

In Defence of the Dog, John Bradshaw

Perfect Puppy, Gwen Bailey

Puppy Training for Children, Sarah Whitehead

Reaching the Animal Mind, Karen Pryor

The Complete Dog Breed Guide, DK

The Dog Encyclopedia, DK

The Puppy Survival Guide, Sarah Whitehead

Think Dog: An Owner's Guide to Canine Psychology, John Fisher

PICTURE CREDITS

The publisher and production company would like to thank the following photographers;

Amabel Adcock – page 7 (left), 16, 23, 38, 50 (right), 139 (bottom left).

Adrian Baughan – page 8, (bottom middle, bottom right), 9 (bottom middle), 12 (middle), 13, 19, 27, 33, 34, 39, 41, 42, 47, 49 (right), 50 (bottom left), 59, 62, 72, 74, 82 (top left), 90, 91, 100, 106, 109, 111, 130, 132, 133.

Ralph Bower – page 7 (bottom right), 54, 69, 139 (bottom right).

Pete Chinn – page 12 (left), 84, 138 (middle).

Adam Heritage – page 2, 7 (top right), 8 (bottom left and top right), 9 (middle top and right), 25, 28, 31, 45, 49 (left), 61, 66, 71, 79, 83, 95 (bottom right), 96, 103, 105, 120, 123, 127, 138 (left, top right and bottom right).

Dan Miller – cover and backcover. Page 8 (top left), 14, 32, 58, 64, 73, 80 (right), 82 (right), 92, 95 (top right), 110, 114, 119, 134, 139 (top left and top right).

Yellow Dog Photography – page 9 (top left), 80 (left), 88, 118, 121.

Ben Tutton – page 30, 139 (top middle).

Chris Vile – page 24.

INDEX

First published in the United Kingdom in 2016 by
Pavilion
1 Gower Street
London
WC1E 6HD

ISBN 978-1-91121-641-4

A CIP catalogue record for this book is available from the British Library.

10 9 8 7 6 5 4 3 2 1

Reproduction by ColourDepth, UK
Printed and bound by GPS Group, Slovenia

This book can be ordered direct from the publisher at
www.pavilionbooks.com

PUBLISHERS' THANKS

We would like to thank Brook Lapping for creating this book with us, special thanks to Andrew McKerlie, Lucy van Beek, Lucy Haken, Rita Ribas, Eilis Barrett and Emily Blackwell. Thanks to Sarah Whitehead, Sarah Hogget and Katie Hewett for your editorial help and Claire Clewley for your beautiful design.

Brook Lapping would like to extend a special thanks to the following owners; Alexandra Mason, Amanda Cordery, Carol Begg, Clair Litster-Huckle, David Lyles, Emma and Richard Parlour, Frank Salmon, Jan Bardey, Jenifer Leo, Laura Ann Mackay, Lorraine Aldcroft, Margo Hackney, Michelle Lorde, Rachel and Michael Cooper, Sheilagh Holmes-Mackie, Tracy Deaker and Wendy Stewart.